SPECTRUM READERS

W9-AUX-097

AWESOME!

 Carson-Dellosa
Publishing

SPECTRUM®

An imprint of Carson-Dellosa Publishing, LLC
P.O. Box 35665
Greensboro, NC 27425-5665

carsondellosa.com

Printed in the USA. All rights reserved.
ISBN 978-1-62399-158-6

01-179137784

WOW!
Big Animals

By Katharine Kenah

Table of Contents

Animals are all around you.
Some animals are
too small to see.
Some animals are big beasts!

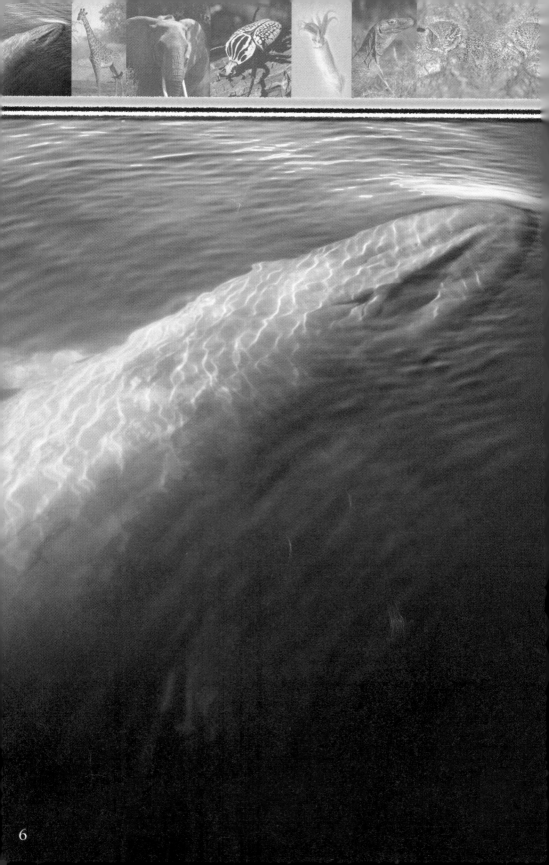

Blue Whale

The blue whale is the biggest
animal in the world.
It is as long as
three school buses.

Giraffe

The giraffe is the tallest
animal in the world.
It is about as tall as
a two-story house.

African Elephant

The African elephant is
the biggest animal on land.
It weighs as much as
two pickup trucks.

Goliath Beetle

The goliath beetle is one of the biggest bugs in the world. It is about as big as your hand.

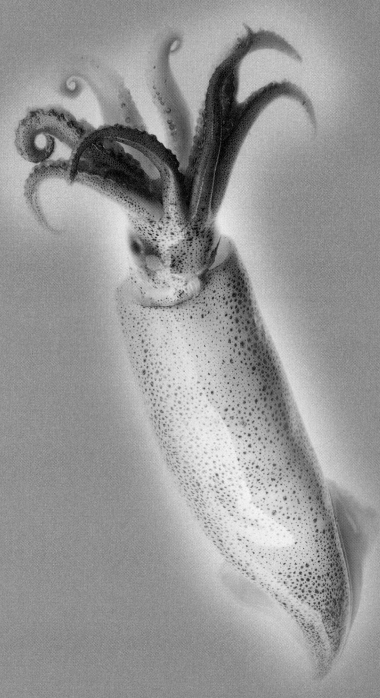

Giant Squid

The giant squid is the biggest
animal with no backbone.
Its eyes are the size
of dinner plates.

Komodo Dragon

The Komodo dragon is
the biggest lizard in the world.
It is longer than
a picnic table.

Crocodile

The crocodile is the biggest reptile in the world.
It is longer than two bikes.

Ostrich

The ostrich is the biggest
bird in the world.
Its eggs are the size
of footballs.

Anaconda

The anaconda is the biggest
snake in the world.
It is about as long
as a garden hose.

Saint Bernard

The Saint Bernard is one of the biggest dogs in the world. It weighs as much as a full-grown man.

Siberian Tiger

The Siberian tiger is
the biggest cat in the world.
It is as long as two bathtubs.

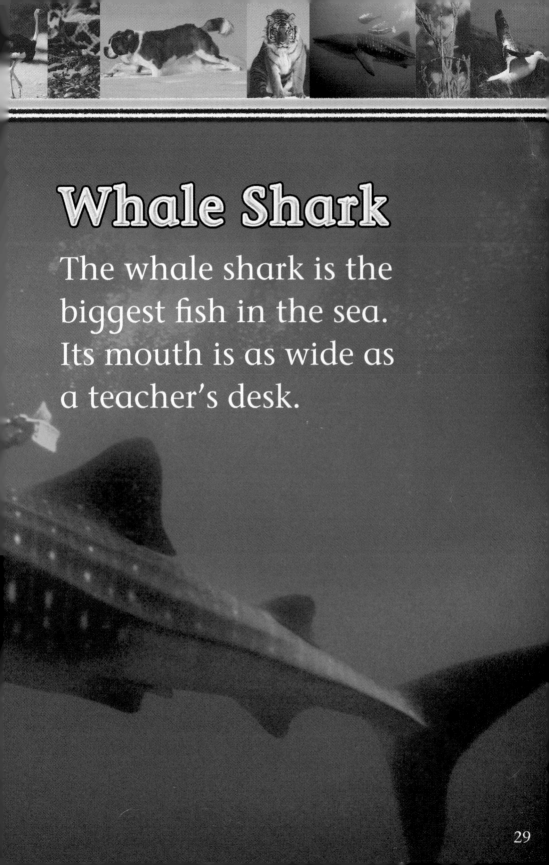

Whale Shark

The whale shark is the biggest fish in the sea. Its mouth is as wide as a teacher's desk.

Stick Insect

The stick insect is the longest insect in the world. It is about as long as a ruler.

Albatross

The albatross is one
of the biggest seabirds.
Its spread wings are about
as wide as a two-lane road.

WOW! Big Animals
Comprehension Questions

1. What is the biggest animal in the world? How long is it?

2. How much does an African elephant weigh? Where do you think it might live?

3. Where do you think the giant squid lives?

4. Which do you think is longer: The world's biggest lizard or the world's biggest reptile?

5. What is an anaconda?

6. Do you think a Saint Bernard weighs more or less than you?

7. About how long is a stick insect?

8. What do you think is the smallest animal in this book?

ODD!
Birds

By Teresa Domnauer

Table of Contents

Some birds are noisy.
Some birds are tiny.
Some birds are colorful.
And some birds are just odd!

Ostrich

This odd bird is an ostrich.
It grows taller than
most people.

Hummingbird

This odd bird is
a hummingbird.
It lays eggs the size
of jelly beans.

Vulture

This odd bird is a vulture.
It eats dead animals.

Snowy Owl

This odd bird is a snowy owl.
Its feathers turn from brown to
white in the winter.

Pelican

This odd bird is a pelican. It uses its pouch like a net to scoop up fish.

Toucan

This odd bird is a toucan.
It has a large
rainbow-colored bill.

Peacock

This odd bird is a peacock.
Its tail feathers make
a beautiful fan.

Flamingo

This odd bird is a flamingo. Its feathers turn pink from the pink shrimp it eats.

Parrot

This odd bird is a parrot.
It can say words—just like
a person.

Blue-Footed Booby

This odd bird is
a blue-footed booby.
It has bright blue legs
and feet.

Arctic Tern

This odd bird is
an arctic tern.
It flies from the North Pole
to the South Pole and back
each year.

Emperor Penguin

This odd bird is
an emperor penguin.
It is taller and heavier than all
other penguins.

Mockingbird

This odd bird is
a mockingbird.
It copies the songs
of other birds.

Roadrunner

This odd bird is a roadrunner.
It runs on land more than
it flies in the air.

ODD! Birds
Comprehension Questions

1. Do you think an ostrich is taller or shorter than you?

2. How big are a hummingbird's eggs?

3. What does a vulture eat?

4. Why do you think a snowy owl's feathers turn white in the winter?

5. Where might you see a pelican?

6. Why are a flamingo's feathers pink?

7. How is a parrot similar to a person?

8. Why do you think the blue-footed booby was given its name?

9. How is an emperor penguin different from other penguins?

LOOK!
Nature's Helpers

By Katharine Kenah

Table of Contents

Some living things
work in pairs.
They help each other.
They are nature's
amazing partners.

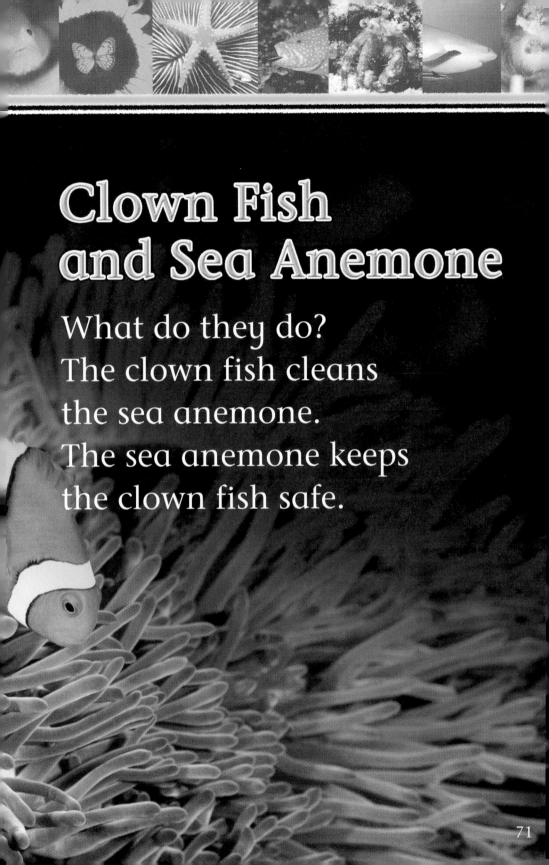

Clown Fish and Sea Anemone

What do they do?
The clown fish cleans
the sea anemone.
The sea anemone keeps
the clown fish safe.

Tickbird and Rhinoceros

What do they do?
The tickbird keeps the
rhinoceros free of bugs.
The rhinoceros keeps the
tickbird full of food.

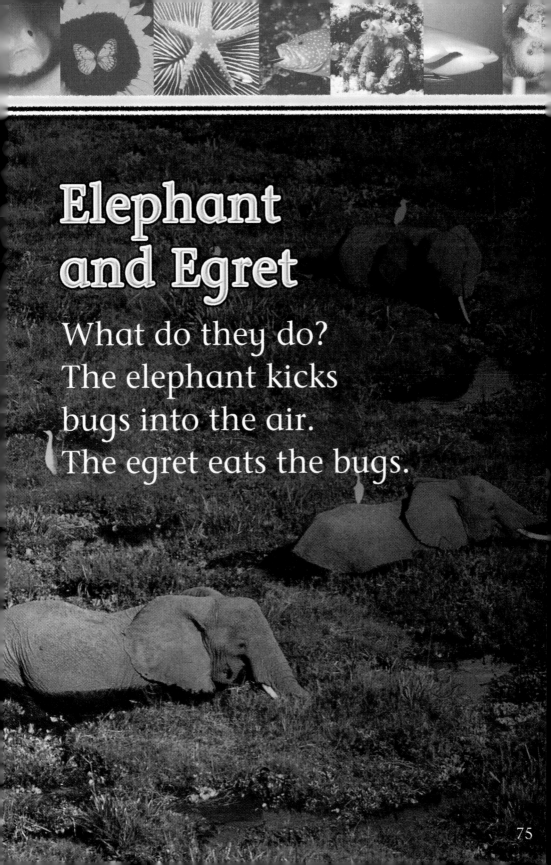

Elephant and Egret

What do they do?
The elephant kicks
bugs into the air.
The egret eats the bugs.

Pitcher Plant and Tree Frog

What do they do?
The pitcher plant draws
in bugs with its colors.
The tree frog eats the bugs.

Plover and Crocodile

What do they do?
The plover cleans out food
from the crocodile's teeth.
The crocodile gives the plover
food to eat.

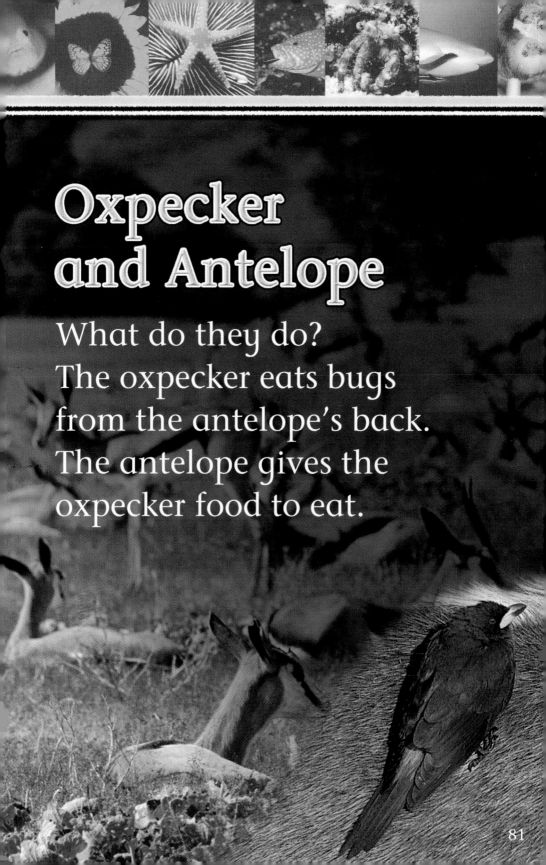

Oxpecker and Antelope

What do they do?
The oxpecker eats bugs
from the antelope's back.
The antelope gives the
oxpecker food to eat.

Flower and Hummingbird

What do they do?
The flower has food
for the hummingbird.
The hummingbird helps
more flowers to grow.

Goby and Sea Urchin

What do they do?
The goby helps the
sea urchin find food.
The sea urchin helps
the goby stay safe.

Sunflower and Butterfly

What do they do?
The sunflower has
food for the butterfly.
The butterfly helps more
sunflowers to grow.

Coral and Starfish

What do they do?
The coral houses
many small animals.
The starfish eats
these animals.

Wrasse and Grouper

What do they do?
The wrasse cleans bugs
from the grouper.
The grouper gives the
wrasse food to eat.

92

Hermit Crab and Sea Anemone

What do they do?
The hermit crab helps the
sea anemone find food.
The sea anemone makes
the hermit crab hard to see.

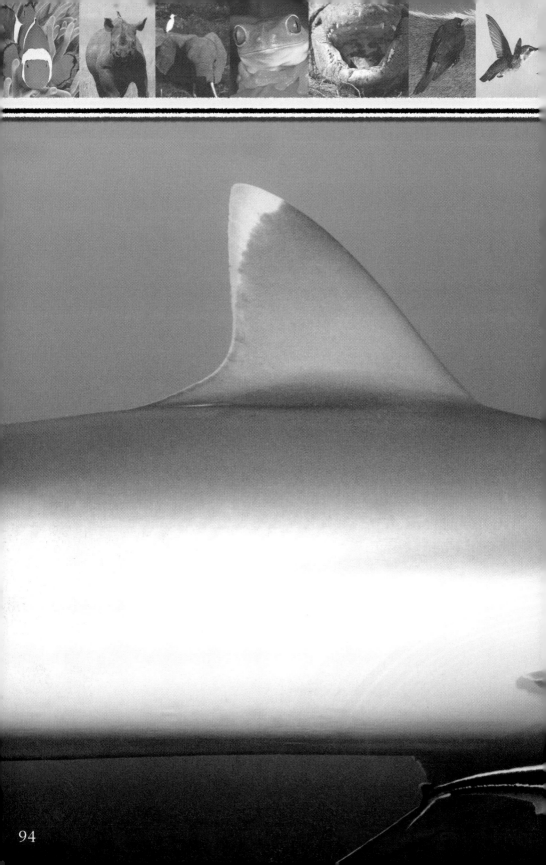

Shark and Remora

What do they do?
The shark gives the
remora a free ride.
The remora eats the food
that the shark does not.

Algae and Sloth

What do they do?
The sloth uses the green
algae to hide in a tree.
The algae grows well
in the sloth's fur.

LOOK! Nature's Helpers Comprehension Questions

1. What does it mean for animals to work in pairs?

2. How does a clown fish help a sea anemone?

3. Why do you think the tickbird needs the rhinoceros?

4. How does the elephant help the egret?

5. How does a pitcher plant draw in bugs?

6. Why do you think the crocodile needs the plover?

7. What do you think would happen if the antelope did not have the oxpecker as a partner?

8. How does the butterfly help the sunflower?

Guided Reading Level: E

SHH!
Night Animals

By Katharine Kenah

Table of Contents

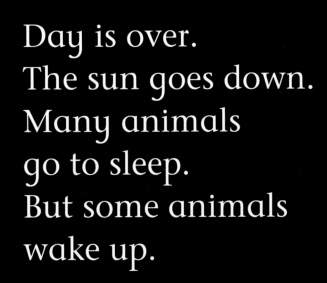

Day is over.
The sun goes down.
Many animals
go to sleep.
But some animals
wake up.

Koala

By day, a koala
sleeps in a tree.
At night, it eats
tree leaves.

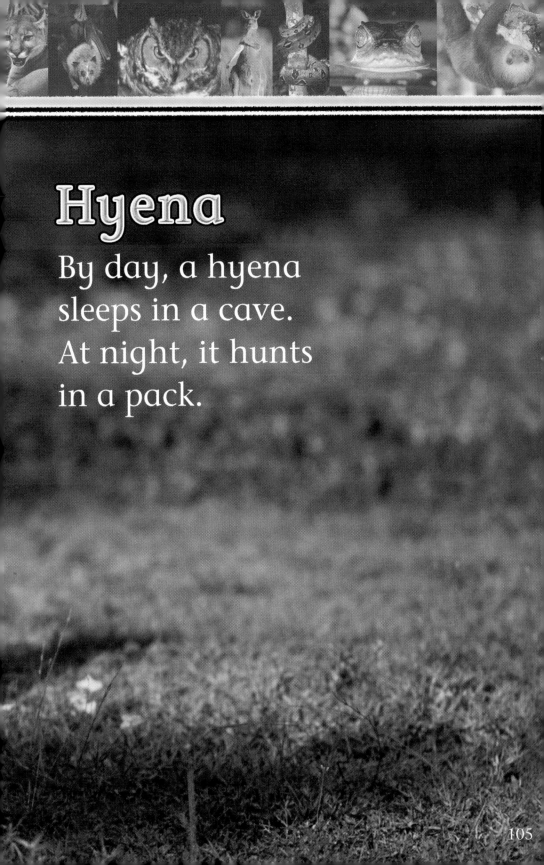

Hyena

By day, a hyena
sleeps in a cave.
At night, it hunts
in a pack.

Opossum

By day, an opossum swings from a tree. At night, it looks for food to eat.

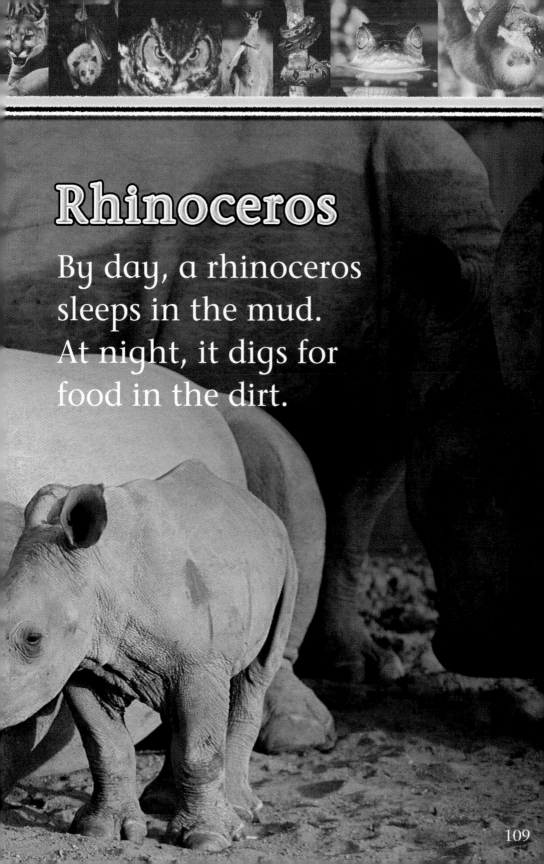

Rhinoceros

By day, a rhinoceros
sleeps in the mud.
At night, it digs for
food in the dirt.

Skunk

By day, a skunk
sleeps in a hole.
At night, it looks
for food to eat.

Sun Bear

By day, a sun bear
sleeps in the sun.
At night, it eats
bugs and honey.

Red Fox

By day, a red fox
sleeps in a den.
At night, it digs
for food in the dirt.

Cougar

By day, a cougar
sleeps in the hills.
At night, it looks
for animals to eat.

Fruit Bat

By day, a fruit bat
hangs from a tree.
At night, it eats fruit.

Owl

By day, an owl
sits in a tree.
At night, it looks
for mice to eat.

Kangaroo

By day, a kangaroo
sleeps in a cool place.
At night, it eats
small plants.

Boa Constrictor

By day, a boa constrictor
sleeps in a tree.
At night, it eats its
food whole!

Caiman

By day, a caiman
stays in the water.
At night, it looks
for food to eat.

Two-Toed Sloth

By day, a sloth
sleeps in a tree.
At night, it eats
fruit and leaves.

SHH! Night Animals
Comprehension Questions

1. Why do you think some animals sleep during the day?

2. What animal swings from a tree during the day?

3. Why do you think a rhinoceros sleeps in the mud?

4. What kind of food do you think the rhinoceros finds in the dirt?

5. What animal eats bugs and honey?

6. Why do you think the fruit bat was given its name?

7. What does an owl do by day?

8. What does a boa constrictor do by night?

9. Where does a two-toed sloth sleep?

Guided Reading Level: E

WACKY!
Pets

By Teresa Domnauer

Table of Contents

Many people have pets. Some people have pets that look very different from most!

Afghan Hound

An Afghan hound
is a kind of dog.
It has a long nose
and long, silky hair.

Mini Hedgehog

A mini hedgehog
has pointy quills.
It can roll up
into a ball.

Rat

A rat is a smart
and clean animal.
A pet rat will sit
in its owner's hands.

Chinchilla

A chinchilla is
soft and furry.
It has big round
ears and eyes.

Gray Parrot

A gray parrot is
a large bird.
It can say words
just like a person!

Green Budgie

A green budgie
is a small parrot.
It can learn to sit
on a person's finger.

Potbellied Pig

A potbellied pig has
a big belly and short legs.
It eats a lot.

Chameleon

A chameleon is
a kind of lizard.
Its skin can
change color.

Boa Constrictor

A boa constrictor is
a big snake.
It can weigh up to
50 pounds!

Green Iguana

A green iguana is
a kind of lizard.
It has pointy scales
on its back.

Leopard Gecko

A leopard gecko has
dark spots.
It can live
for 30 years!

Hermit Crab

A hermit crab has
one big claw.
It finds a shell
and lives inside.

Tarantula

A tarantula is
a hairy spider.
It can be as big
as a hand!

Pet Care

All pets need care.
They need food, water,
and a place to live.
It is good to learn a lot
about a pet before you
bring it home!

WACKY! Pets
Comprehension Questions

1. Why do you think many people have pets?

2. Do you think a mini hedgehog would be a good pet? Why or why not?

3. What are two words that describe a rat?

4. How is a gray parrot like a person?

5. What is a green budgie?

6. Why do you think the potbellied pig was given its name?

7. How much does a boa constrictor weigh?

8. How is a leopard gecko similar to a leopard?

9. Which of these pets would you most like to have? Why?

Guided Reading Level: G

COOL!
Sea Life

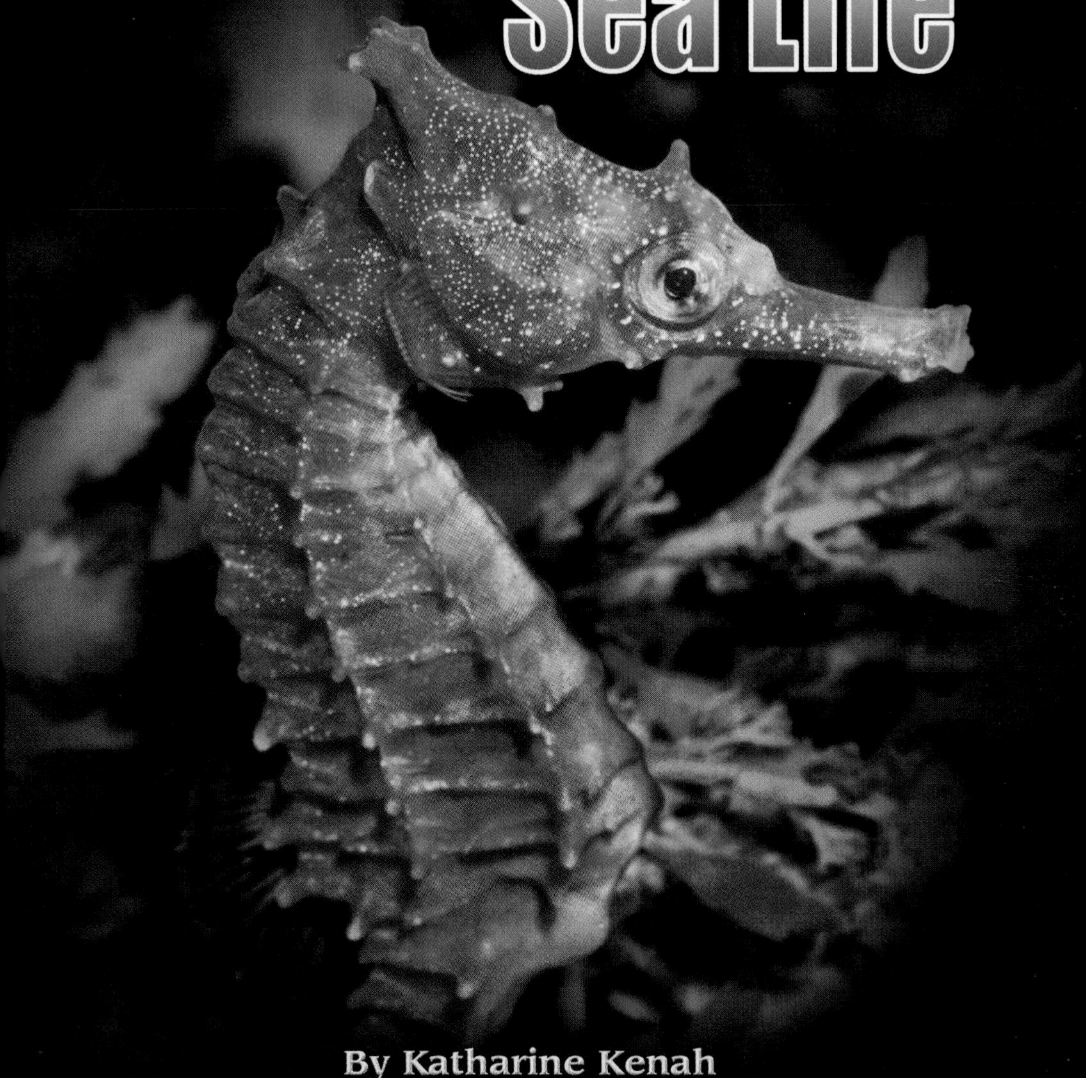

By Katharine Kenah

Table of Contents

The sun is warm.
The water is blue.
People swim at the top
of the sea.
Creatures of the deep
swim below.

Manatee

A manatee is called a *sea cow*. It moves slowly in the water and eats plants.

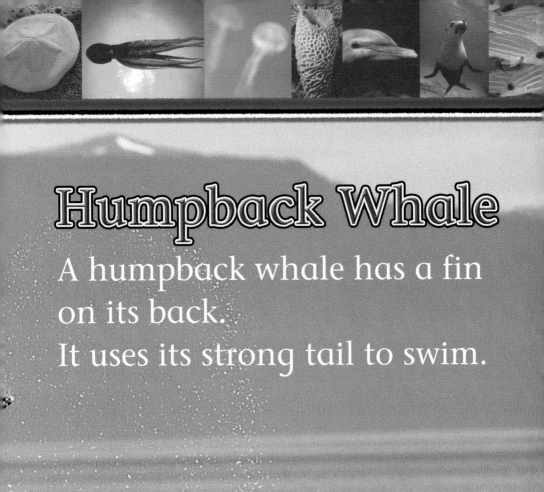

Humpback Whale

A humpback whale has a fin on its back.

It uses its strong tail to swim.

Great White Shark

A great white shark is big
and strong.
It has lots of sharp teeth.

Crab

A crab has a hard shell.
It has eight legs and
two claws.

Sea Horse

A sea horse has a
strong tail.
Its head looks like
a horse's head.

Hammerhead Shark

A hammerhead shark has eyes
on the sides of its head.
It finds food that is far away.

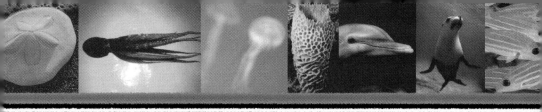

Eel

An eel hides in
a hole underwater.
It waits for a fish
to eat.

Sand Dollar

A sand dollar is
as big as a cookie.
It moves and digs
in the sand.

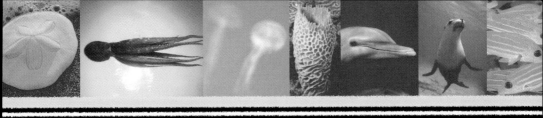

Octopus

An octopus has three hearts and eight arms.
It uses its arms to find food.

Jellyfish

A jellyfish has a soft body.
It can sting fish that
swim nearby.

Sponge

A sponge looks like a plant, but it is an animal. It has no head!

Dolphin

A dolphin is a small whale.
It swims and dives
in the water.

Sea Lion

A sea lion is a seal with ears.
It swims in the water and
rests on rocks.

School of Fish

A group of the same fish is called a *school*. The fish swim in the sea together.

COOL! Sea Life
Comprehension Questions

1. Which animal is called a sea cow? Why do you think it was given that nickname?

2. Why do you think the sea horse has a strong tail? What do you think it uses its tail for?

3. Why do you think the sea horse was given its name?

4. Why do you think the hammerhead shark is called "hammerhead"?

5. Where else might you see a sponge?

6. Do eels remind you of an animal that you might see on land? Which one?

7. Which animal has three hearts?

Guided Reading Level: F

AWESOME!
Snakes

By Teresa Domnauer

Table of Contents

They slither.
They crawl.
They climb trees.
They hunt and swim.
Warning: amazing snakes
ahead!

Egyptian Cobra

Snakes can curl into a circle.
Scales cover their bodies.

Green Viper

Snakes have tongues that
look like forks.
Their tongues help them
smell enemies and find food

Rattlesnake

Snakes have special ways
to stay safe.
This snake shakes its tail.
The sound tells enemies
to stay away.

Black Cobra

This snake lifts up its body
to look bigger.
This keeps away some
of its enemies.

Emerald Tree Boa

Some snakes can climb trees. This snake's color helps it hide in the leaves.

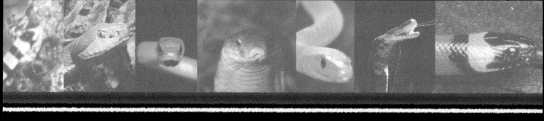

Burmese Python

Some snakes live in warm places.
This snake lives in a tropical rain forest.

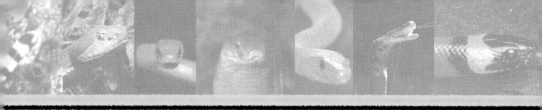

Sand Viper

Some snakes live in hot deserts.
This snake hides in the desert sand.

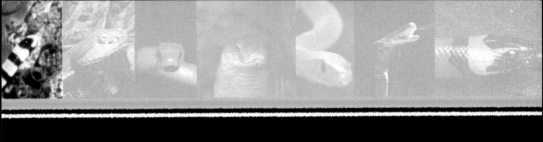

Yellow-Lip
Sea Snake

Other snakes live in
the ocean.
This snake has a flat tail.

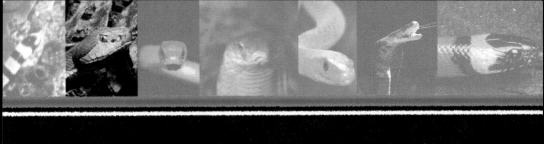

Copperhead

Snakes hunt for food.
They swallow it whole!
This snake eats mice
and frogs.

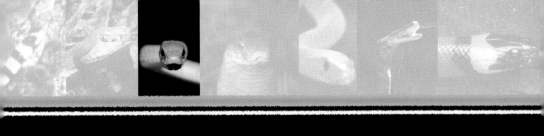

Natal Green Snake

Some snakes, like this one,
hunt at night.
They rest during the day.

King Brown Snake

Snakes live all over
the world.
This snake lives in Australia.

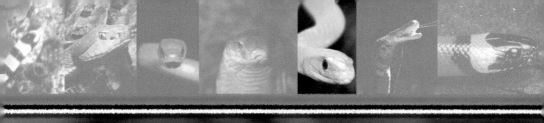

Green Mamba

This snake lives in Africa.
It has a very dangerous bite.
Poison, called *venom*, comes
out of its fangs.

Spitting Cobra

This snake has dangerous venom, too.
It can spit the venom over six feet.

Milk Snake

This snake is not harmful at all.
But enemies stay away from it.
It looks just like a dangerous snake.

AWESOME! Snakes
Comprehension Questions

1. How do snakes use their tongues?

2. What does it mean when a rattlesnake shakes its tail?

3. Why does the black cobra lift up its body?

4. Where does the Burmese python live?

5. Why does the yellow-lip sea snake have a flat tail?

6. How does a snake eat its food?

7. Where does the king brown snake live?

8. Do you think you would like to see a green mamba in the wild? Why or why not?

9. What is venom? Name two snakes that have venom.

ALERT!

Wild Weather

Table of Contents

Weather is all around you.
Some weather is hot.
Some weather is cold.
And some weather is wild!

Storm Cloud

This is a storm cloud. Storm clouds are filled with drops of water.

Lightning

This is lightning.
Lightning flashes in the sky.

Rain

This is rain.
Drops of water
fall from a cloud.

Flood

This is a flood.
Too much rain
brings a flood.

Drought

This is a drought.
Too little rain makes
a drought.

Dust Storm

This is a dust storm.
Dust storms fill the
air with dirt and sand.

Fog

This is fog.
Fog is a cloud that
is on the ground.

Rainbow

This is a rainbow. Rainbows are made when the sun shines through raindrops.

Hail

This is hail.
Hail is made of
tiny balls of ice.

Snow

This is snow.
No two snowflakes
are the same.

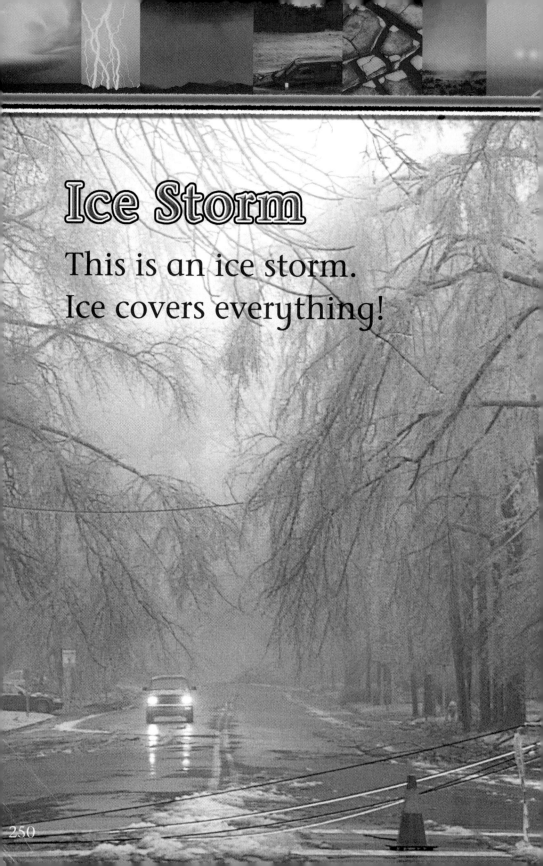

Ice Storm

This is an ice storm.
Ice covers everything!

Tornado

This is a tornado.
Tornados are storms
with very strong winds.

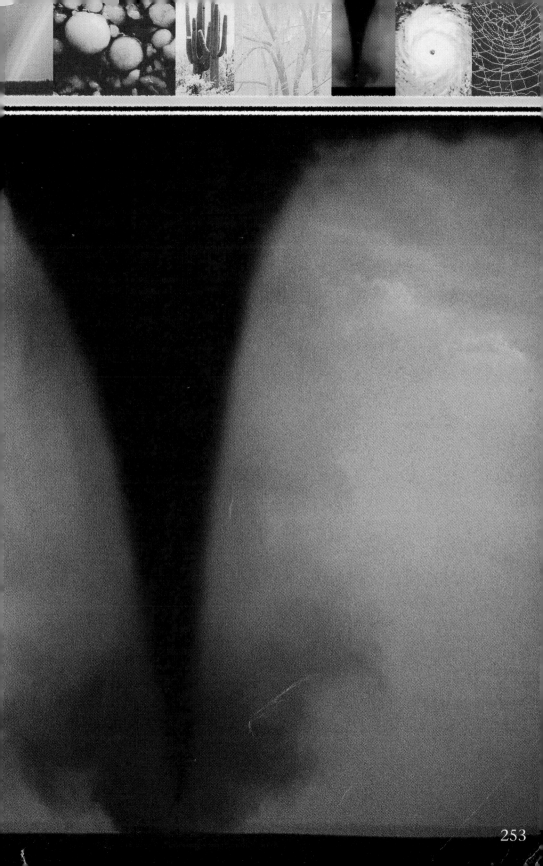

Hurricane

This is a hurricane.
Hurricanes are big
storms from the sea.

ALERT! Wild Weather Comprehension Questions

1. When are you most likely to see lightning?

2. Why is rain a good thing? When can it be a bad thing?

3. What causes a flood?

4. What causes a drought?

5. What is fog?

6. Can you name the colors in a rainbow?

7. When might you see a rainbow?

8. In which season are you most likely to see hail?

9. What is a tornado? Use two words to describe a tornado.

10. What is the weather like today? Use two words to describe it.